Pathways of Recovery

New Life for the Diminished Person

James A. Kitchens, Ph.D.

ADS-CO., INC.
Dallas, Texas

Pathways of Recovery: New Life for the Diminished Person ©1990 by James A. Kitchens, Ph.D.
ISBN 0-9624469-1-2

ADS-CO, INC.
4213 Wiley Post
Dallas, Texas 75244
(214) 387-4733

PATHWAYS OF RECOVERY

Diseases desperate grown
By *desperate appliances are relieved,*
Or *not at all.*

William Shakespeare

*To Rachel, companion and
friend as I walk my pathway.*

Contents

Introduction

Do You:

Yes No

□ □ Dislike yourself as you are?

□ □ Frequently wish you were like someone else?

□ □ Have trouble developing intimate relationships?

□ □ Feel insecure and uncertain?

□ □ Have trouble with alcohol or other drugs?

□ □ Struggle with anger, fear, and self-doubt?

□ □ Have trouble knowing what you want?

□ □ Feel grateful when someone is nice to you?

□ □ Deny the truth so people will like you?

□ □ Have trouble controlling sexual urges?

□ □ Find it impossible to express your sexuality in healthy ways?

□ □ Fear that people do not like you?

□ □ Let other people's problems snag your life?

□ □ Have trouble trusting people?

□ □ Have poor communication skills?

□ □ Feel alone and lonely most of the time?

If you checked yes to three or more of these questions, this book is for you. Welcome. You are part of a large group, a group of us who for whatever reason are not able to fulfill the unique potential which allows us to live the fullest possible life. In fact we may not even be able to perceive that potential in us because we do not know our-

1

selves that well. We are emotionally stunted and end up shortchanged by life.

Diminished is a good name by which to describe people like us. It comes from the Latin *minuere,* which means to make smaller. We get the words miniature, minuscule, and minus from this root. As diminished people, we sense ourselves reduced in degree of importance and as somehow smaller or less than other people. We feel ineffectual in dealing with the demands of life, like everyone else is competent and we are inept. For some reason, we can't affirm or accept or even understand ourselves.

We are dwarfed in emotions and in behaviors. It is not that we lack accomplishment or that we lead wasted lives in the sense that we end up on skid row or destroy ourselves with some self-destructive habit. While it is true that some of us do end up destroying ourselves with alcohol or other drug abuse and some of us just throw life away and waste it in frivolous pursuits, most of us diminished people are outwardly successful. We manage to hold life together, even get ahead. We don't live in the slums of some inner-city ghetto. We may be either religious or irreligious, or something in between. We can be either young or old, male or female. We don't even always *look* unhappy. In fact, some of us may even lead what appears from the outside to be exciting and glamorous lives. The mark that distinguishes us folk is that regardless of our physical shape or our station in society, we feel that we will never have the things that really count in life and that somehow we will always be *less than others.*

We can empathize with the person that Rachel James describes in her poem, *Paradoxical Embrace.* She says:

> *I am like a beggar,*
> *A beggar for Life,*
> *Running from person to person,*
> *   idea to idea,*
> *Raising my hands in anguished*
> *   supplication, searching*

And the smiling faces neither see
nor hear me; but continue
To revel in the secret of Life
Their eyes averted from me.

Pecola Breedlove, the child in Toni Morrison's moving novel, *The Bluest Eye*, is an extreme example of the diminished person. Throughout her childhood, Pecola felt that there was no one who noticed, or loved, or cared about her. There was nothing about her that caught people's attention. But, she thought, if I had blue eyes, everything would be different. Then I would be unique and my parents would stop fighting. Then I would be beautiful and my father would stop drinking. Then I would be special and everyone would love me. In short, Pecola concluded, if I were not me, everything would be okay. Or, turned around, if I were like someone else, things would go smoothly and I could get what I want. Life had diminished Pecola because she suffered from the greatest human despair —she could not be herself.

What It Means To Be A Diminished Person

Being diminished means that we never fulfill the promise bundled up inside of us as infants. We never get to be what we truly are and end up missing the total joy and satisfaction for which we were created. We are like a seed dropped into unprepared soil, soil that is rocky or shaded by weeds or lacking proper nutrients or sufficient moisture. This unfortunate environment produces a plant which is stunted and lives a weakened and impoverished existence. This plant comes nowhere near developing the potential contained in the germinated seed.

Very few of us having grown up in America have not in some important way suffered from the impact of an environment which diminishes us and keeps us from being what we truly are. Ours is a culture in which the social and psychological context hardly ever provides the atmosphere in which members have their needs as humans met.

The family has gone haywire, largely having lost its traditional functions and today most children must survive what frankly are families that are basically dysfunctional. That is the point of many of the cartoons which poke fun at today's family. For example, there's the joke about the man who tells his psychiatrist, "I grew up in a bad neighborhood; my parents lived there."

But it is not just the family. Most of the institutions that are responsible for the rearing of children in today's world frequently do more harm than good. The child must suffer the indignity of dysfunctional schools, dysfunctional communities, dysfunctional churches, dysfunctional television, dysfunctional peer groups, and dysfunctional recreation. In short, our total environment is inhumane because it does not provide the elements necessary to allow our basic humanity to develop to its fullest. Just as the plant cursed with an insufficient environment cannot get what it needs to grow up strong and productive, we are lost in an environment that denies us the basic nutrients for healthy growth and development.

From time to time we read in our newspaper about an animal that has been penned in insufficient space and denied proper nutrition and care. Pictures show the animal as gaunt, emaciated, and wasted away by the ordeal. It is but a shadow of its original self. Diminished people are like that on the inside. Our sense of worth is shriveled beyond recognition. Denied the fulfillment of our basic needs, we are emotionally stunted. It is like being imprisoned in a smaller self, a delimited self. The diminished person may empathize with the writer in the New Testament who admitted that he found himself doing those things which he wished not to do and unable to do those things for which he truly longed. We feel that we are not really in control of our lives.

A number of terms are being used today to describe people who suffer these and similar problems. We are being called co-dependent, adult children of dysfunctional families, addicted personalities, and wounded children. Some members of the American Psychiatric Association have diagnosed us as suffering from Personality Disorders of various kinds. Whatever the term, the syndrome is always the same. We are less than what we could be, we lack the joy of controlling our lives, we feel less than others, we fear being discovered as impostors, we never have the genuine intimacy we wish for, we have habits we can't break and goals we can't accomplish, and we hide from others and ultimately from ourselves. Sometimes we even wish that life would hurry up and end.

The Basic Human Needs

As noted, the fundamental needs of the diminished person have gone unmet. And what are the needs which have been denied to the diminished person? Beyond the basic physical needs for food and shelter, every person needs the following for normal development of mental wholeness:

WHAT EVERY CHILD (and adult) NEEDS

Security "I belong here and I am safe."

Love "I really matter to someone."

Acceptance "I am liked just the way I am." "I am accepted even though the things I do are not all accepted."

Boundaries "There are fair limits to what I am allowed to do. Someone will help me stay within those limits."

Guidance "I will have help in learning how to behave and what to do."

Independence "I will be encouraged to try new things by myself."

Discipline "Someone will have the strength to tell me when I do something wrong and will encourage me to do it right."

Modeling "Someone will show me how to express feelings openly, how to communicate directly, and how to ask for what I need."

Forgiveness "I will not always be what I am expected to be. When I am not, the people I love will forgive me."

Acknowledgement "I am truly unique. There is no one like me in the world. Someone will say thanks to me for being me."

The Human Loss Of Humanness

When we grow up in an atmosphere which blocks the fulfillment of these basic needs, we have trouble being human. That is, we cannot be those things which a human is created to be. Again, we are like a plant. Denied proper provisions for normal development, it cannot be what a plant is supposed to be. It does not look like a normal plant and it does not do what a normal plant does. Its fruit, if there is any, is usually small and incomplete. So with us humans. Not having developed properly, we find it difficult to be those things which a healthy human is supposed to be. We have trouble answering the basic questions of human life:

• Who am I? That is, we have a hard time perceiving or knowing ourselves.

• What is my value? We feel that we have no intrinsic value and thus try to become valuable by performance of some kind. Usually we try to perform in areas which we think others expect from us. We find it impossible in this context to love and affirm ourselves. We feel like we are impostors and spend our life trying to keep other people from finding out that we are fake.

• Who am I with? Diminished children always grow up having trouble with relationships and especially with intimate relationships. For us, risk and vulnerability are overpowering and we avoid them at all costs. In their place, we put control and manipulation.

• What do I do? We have a hard time knowing
what we are for. We have trouble with basic life
skills and with vocational goals. We feel lost
most of the time as if we had no destination. Or,
if we do have a destination, we feel behind and
are desperate to catch up.
• What does my life mean? Questions of the
meaning of life, its purpose, and our reason for
being are very difficult for us to answer. We
want to count for something and have signif-
icance in our lives. What we feel instead is mean-
ingless and somehow estranged even from ourselves.

Pathways To Recovery

But I do not want us to despair. Just as the emaciated
animal and the stunted plant may be nurtured back to
health, so recovery is possible for the diminished person.
We can, with proper care, return to health and growth.
We can become productive and happy and fulfilled persons. Recovery moves us slowly along toward the following characteristics of mental wholeness.

The recovering person is *self-affirming*. Mentally healthy persons see themselves as they are
and like what they see. They have accurate self-
perception. They know their limitations and
they accept them without self-loathing. They
seek to improve because they want to grow and
self-actualize, not because they are ashamed of
what they are. Mentally healthy people laugh a
lot and do not take themselves too seriously.

The recovering person is able to *make choices*
and *accept losses*. The mentally healthy person
sees choices in life and is able to make them.
Once made, the healthy person does not go
back and second-guess the decisions. Further,

undiminished persons can handle loss. They
grieve fully, going through the full cycle of pain,
and then go on with life.

The recovering person is *gentle*. Gentle people
do not require that things be one way. They are
flexible and can be comfortable with the paradoxical. Further, gentleness is the opposite of
control and manipulation. It is honest and direct.
It neither deceives nor is it deceived.

The recovering person is *trusting*. Mentally healthy
people demand the truth in themselves and in
others. This means that they are vulnerable
because they do not avoid truth in themselves
and in others. They treat themselves and others
fairly and equally. This quality means that the
mentally healthy person is seeking truth in the
sense that he or she does not already *know* it.
They are open to discovery in others and in
themselves. To be trusting means that they can
be dependent and weak when it is appropriate.

The recovering person is *merciful*. To be merciful is to refuse to be judgmental. This does not
mean that mentally healthy people are not dis-
cerning and that they do not evaluate people
because they refuse to recognize faults and see
other people's defects. Rather, it means that
they do not discriminate unfairly. And they do
not use other people's weaknesses as a tool to
embarrass, hurt, or control.

The recovering person is *congruent*. The word
congruence means to "come together." Congruent people are people who "have it all together." Congruence means that what is inside

is what they present to other people. That is, undiminished people are congruent because they know what is inside them and they are not ashamed. They have no need to have secrets about themselves and they can choose to whom they will reveal these secrets.

The recovering person *seeks peaceful, loving, and healthy relationships.* This quality does not mean that he or she avoids conflict or is afraid of confrontation. Seeking peaceful and loving relationships may sometimes mean being confrontive. Neither does it mean that the person wants only harmony. Peace is much like serenity in this sense. That is, it is the the opposite of disorder. Mentally healthy people seek to establish order, communication, understanding, and cooperation between themselves and other people.

The recovering person is capable of *commitment.* Healthy people have things in which they are interested that are bigger than they are. The commitment is found in that they are attracted to these things and are captivated by them. Mentally healthy persons seek relationships, causes, and involvements to which they may give themselves. For them life is more than simple hedonistic enjoyment. At the same time, mentally healthy people are able to say when they have made a mistake and to express their desire to get out of a commitment.

How To Use This Book

So, if you suffer because you are a diminished person, this little book is for you. And here is how to use it.

Doing the exercises.

1. It is better if you do the excercises in the sequence in which they are presented. Do not skip around.

2. It is better to do the excercises slowly, no more than one a day and preferably no more than one a week. This pace allows you time to prepare to do each exercise and then to deal in depth with what the exercise brings up.

3. Before doing the exercise, read it over and ponder the subject it covers. Be aware of the feelings you have as you contemplate doing the exercise. Are you excited and eager to do it? Does it fill you with anticipation as you see yourself answering the questions? Or, does it bring a sense of hesitation and dread as you consider the topic under consideration? Ask yourself why you have these feelings.

4) After spending time thinking about the exercise, begin to record your answers to the questions posed in the exercise. Write out your answers to each question as completely as you wish. Do the exercises only to the detail that satisfies you. Use extra paper if necessary. Make the pictures as fancy and detailed as you please. Stick figures will suffice or, if you prefer, carefully drawn and precise representations are permissible.

5) Each exercise is followed by a section entitled, "For Reflection and Discussion." It includes a list of questions which are designed to stimulate your thinking after the exercise is done and to keep you concentrating on the issues which the exercise has uncovered. Let your mind roam over them as you go about your daily activities. Some of these sections also include brief comments by diminished persons which are incorporated to encourage your thinking and to serve as examples for you. A few contain cartoons which illustrate some aspect of the recovery process. After you have thought through these matters, you may wish to discuss them, and the exercises, with a safe friend or in a small group.

The object of the exercises is to allow you to get material from your unconscious, your deep inner mind, up to the conscious level. These issues have festered below the surface, sometimes since infancy and childhood, like a cancer which is unseen but deadly. What the exercises do is push them from their hiding place to the light of day where you can understand better what is going on. You get a better grasp of yourself in the process and can comprehend you and your life more adequately.

There are a number of excellent companion books which you may wish to read as you work your way through these exercises. Among them are *Codependent No More* and *Beyond Codependency*, by Melody Beattie; *Adult Children of Alcoholics* and *Struggle For Intimacy*, by Janet Woititz; *Facing Codependence*, by Pia Mellody; *Out Of The Shadows*, by Patrick Carnes; *The Flying Boy*, by John Lee; *Healing The Child Within*, by Charles Whitfield; *The Dance Of Anger*, by Harriet Lerner; and *It Will Never Happen To Me*, by Claudia Black.

What we are looking for is *self-understanding*, not blame. While we will spend time in these exercises looking at how other people have hurt us, we do not do this in order to condemn others or to fix guilt on someone else for our shortcomings. To the contrary, we are trying to understand how we got the way we are in order to *take responsibility for ourselves*. Beyond the increased self-understanding, the process helps us develop more adequate and healthy coping mechanisms. In such a way we begin to change our life. In short, we have greater control over ourselves and find that we are gradually understanding, accepting, and liking ourselves more.

Sharing in a support group.
   If possible, you may wish to do the exercises in a group, or at least with another person or two. Groups are strengthening to us because we not only get the results of our work but that of others as well. Seeing how others react helps us to see ourselves better. The following are suggestions to make the group as effective as possible.

   1. The group should range in size from four to eight. Its purpose should be to meet to facilitate growth in all members. There should be a spirit of care and trust and each person must be willing to promise confidentiality to all others in the group.

   2. The group's purpose is personal growth. To a-chieve this goal, each person must restrain from "advice-giving" and "problem-solving." Group members will want to avoid statements like, "Well, what you should do is. . ." or "I think you ought to. . . ." It is best to avoid all shoulds and oughts.

3. The group will function best if it meets for a couple of hours once a week. Designate one exercise that all members will do as homework prior to the group meeting. To get the most from the group, you must be willing to talk about yourself during the group. Share what you get from the exercise. Tell how it illuminates your past, how it helps you see what is going on in your life now, and what it tells you about your hopes and fears about the future. As you do, try to be aware of the here and now. How are others responding to what you are saying? How do you feel about yourself as you talk?

4. Be aware of your feelings during the group meetings. What are your reactions to what others are saying and doing? Don't *control* your feelings; be *aware* of them. Also, try to get a feel for how the group as a whole is reacting.

5. Be willing to share what you are feeling as the group goes along. We all have both positive and negative reactions. Both are important. Talk about both. Try not to be defensive at what others say. Ask them leading questions that give them opportunity to explore themselves at a deeper level. Some suggested questions are: "How do you feel about that?" "Could you tell us more about that?" "What are you feeling as you talk about that now?" We also encourage the other to go deeper with supportive statements like, "I can understand how you would feel that way," and "I believe you."

6. Between meetings think about what happened to you and to others in the group in the last session.

Spend some time each week mulling over where you and the group are.

7. Go slowly and be gentle. Do not expect too much of yourself. Healing is a process and this group is but one step in that direction.

8. Look for changes in your behavior, attitudes, feelings, thoughts, and beliefs. Try out things you learn in the group with safe people. Be aware of your everyday life.

This book includes twenty-six exercises. If you and your group do one a week, you will spend about six months in completing them all. When done, you may wish to start again at the beginning and do them over once more. You will be pleased at how much deeper your understanding will go the second time through. If you follow this procedure, you and your group will spend one year in the process of personal growth.

The Signs Of Recovery

The following are signs of progress which you may wish to look for in yourself:
  • You begin to see more self-awareness and greater self-understanding.
  • You find that you are more self-accepting and you like what you see in yourself.
  • You are more willing to be honest and begin to recognize your denial of reality.
  • You find that you are gradually becoming less responsible for others and more in control of yourself.

- You have more clarity in goals and greater self-understanding in what you are feeling and what you want and need in life.
- You are less negative about life and self and experience less guilt and shame.
- You are more open to positive, creative, and healthy people.
- You experience more positive feelings about life and about yourself.
- You are more able to say "No" without feeling guilty even when it makes others angry or when it inconveniences them.
- You are more able to separate your feelings from others and to claim them as your own.

So. Here you are poised on the brink of a new and significant step in your journey. You are about to do something for yourself, and only for yourself. The pathway that stretches before you leads to health and growth. You are not doing this because you want other people to do something for you or because you are not okay if they do not. You are doing it for you, because you are worth it, and because you are being responsible for you.

This is your *primavera,* the springtime of your life. That which has lain dormant through the long months of deprivation and malnourishment is about to burst forth in life. The branches that you thought were dead have all along been surging with unseen life and now are about to sprout with buds and blossoms. Godspeed.

Part One

FACING
THE PAIN
AND
GRIEVING
THE PAST

The exercises in Part One are designed to help us face the past. That is not as easy as it sounds. There are compelling prohibitions in our society against honestly facing the past. We are told, "Let sleeping dogs lie," and "The past is past, don't stir in it." It would be nice if the past were in fact past, but the sad news is that it is not. Unfortunately, our personal past is not unlike William Faulkner's evaluation of the South. "There are places in the South," he once said, "where past history is not history and neither is it past."

For that reason, we must look squarely at our past even though to do so is always a painful process. Our goal is to wake those sleeping dogs in such a way as to transpose them into harmless puppies.

EXERCISE 1

REALLY, TO KNOW ME IS TO LOVE ME

Let your mind go back to your childhood. Picture the house you lived in, the church you attended, your school, the places you played, the children you played with, your parents' relationship, and other parts of your childhood experience. Let your mind drift easily over these and other things from your life as a child. Even if there was extreme trauma, let your mind take in what happened to you. Close your eyes and see yourself as the child you were. You are safe now and even if it is painful or scary, looking back is healthy as you let these memories come to the surface. Picture yourself doing the childhood things you did. Take your time and try to concentrate on your feelings as well as the experiences you had. When you have taken all the time you wish, go on to the rest of the exercise.

Find a picture taken of you when you were a child and glue it in the space provided below. You may wish to put in several pictures in order to show you at various stages of your childhood. Label each picture and tell why it is significant to you in telling your childhood story. Use extra pages as necessary.

1. Briefly describe yourself physically as a child.

2. List and briefly explain three feelings you had as a child.
    1.

    2.

    3.

3. Draw a picture of your childhood family. Include all persons that played a significant role in your family.

4. Describe your family. How did your parents relate? Who talked to whom? How was affection, anger, and conflict expressed in your family? If you had to pick one word to describe your family, what would that word be?

5. Close your eyes and get a clear picture of this child sitting in the bedroom of the house in which she or he grew up. See yourself as an adult in that room. Try to imagine what the child is feeling and thinking. Walk over and put your arms around the child. Kiss the child on the cheek. Call the child by name and say, "I love you and I will always be here for you. If you wish, you may come with me out of here." See yourself walking out of the house. Breathe deeply a couple of times and then open your eyes. When you are ready, write out what you saw and what the exercise felt like to you.

FOR REFLECTION AND DISCUSSION

1. What major theme seems to come through for you in this exercise?
2. How did you feel as you were thinking and writing about these things?
3. What would you think a child raised in this atmosphere would think and feel about:
   Herself or himself.
   What family relationships are supposed to be.
   How to make it in the world.
4. What were your feelings as you touched and kissed the child? How did the child react to you? Did the child come with you as you left the house? How can you love and nurture this child today?

EXERCISE 2

GETTING IN TOUCH WITH YOUR LOSSES

Please make a list of five people who have hurt you at some point in the past. These may include people from your childhood as well as your teen years and adult years. List them by name. After each name, write out what these persons did that hurt you. Think in terms of specific behaviors, e.g., "He made fun of me in public situations," "She never said she was proud of me," "He molested me as a child." Avoid statements like, "He made me feel...." Please be as complete as possible. Use extra paper if you need to.

1. _____

2. _____

3. _____

4. _____

5. _____

FOR REFLECTION AND DISCUSSION

1. How did you feel as you thought about doing this exercise? How did you feel while you were doing it?

2. Select one of the persons you wrote about and share what you have written with your discussion group. If you are not in a group, find a safe person (someone who will listen supportively and will not find fault with you nor *give you advice*) and share your experience with this person.

3. Consider the following cartoon. What does it say to you about yourself?

Reprinted with permission of UFS, Inc.

EXERCISE 3

DEALING WITH THE PAIN

In the previous exercise, you made a list of the people who have hurt you and wrote out specific things which they did that were damaging to you. You feel diminished by these experiences and there is much pain in these memories. You may not know what to do with that pain. The experiences hurt originally and it still hurts to remember them. That's the reason why you have tried all these years to bury them. However, remembering them and writing about them is in itself healing. But remembering and feeling the pain is not enough. There is another step for you to take.

So, having brought these memories to the conscious level, I want you to get in touch with what you need to do with this material. Do not waste time thinking about the expectations that other people have of what you should do with these memories. You need no more "shoulds" in your life. Rather, get in touch with your own "deep mind," the inner voice of the loving child in you is what you need to help you with the pain and bitterness. That inner child's voice is healing and will direct you and help you with your grief.

The following guided imagery will help get you to this deep mind.

Find some private place where you will not be disturbed for ten or fifteen minutes. Sit down in a comfortable chair with both feet on the floor, your back straight, and your hands folded in your lap.

Close your eyes and imagine yourself in a broad and beautiful meadow. It is springtime and the sun is warm.

The sky is blue and large fleecy clouds float overhead. The grass is green and the air is full of the smell of fragrant blossoms. You are following a small path that leads toward a hill. In your hands are two heavy suitcases filled with the painful memories about which you have been writing and thinking.

Imagine the sights and sounds as you approach the hill. Feel the sun on your skin. Look at the blue sky and the floating clouds. Hear the wind rustling gently through the trees. Feel the ache in your back as you carry the heavy suitcases.

You are walking up that hill and the path you are following is winding through the beautiful trees. The birds are singing and the smell of the forest is clean and crisp. Up ahead you notice a person sitting near the edge of the path.

This person is
> a trusted and loving old sage
> a good listener
> kind, warm, and affectionate
> someone who sees the good in others
> and very wise.

As you draw even with the seated figure, you see the old sage motion to you by the wave of a hand in a beckoning gesture. You approach and are aware of a gentle and loving smile. You feel very comfortable and safe.

The wise and loving sage speaks:

"The bags look heavy and your arms look weary from carrying them. Place them on the ground and rest a-while."

You put them down and step back, looking into the warm eyes of this loving person.

"These heavy bags must surely contain something important," your kind host says. "What do they contain?"

You answer by describing in detail what is in each bag. You are aware that as you speak, your friend listens intently. You conclude, "I am tired of carrying these old heavy bags. I have carried them for years and I guess I didn't realize that I could set them down for awhile. I do not know what to do with them. Can you help me?"

With a warm smile, the person says, "Yes, I can," and continues to speak, telling you what to do with the material in the bags.

You listen carefully to what the person says.

Having told you what to do, the kind person reaches into a satchel and pulls out a gift for you. You extend your hand and take the gift and look at it. After a moment, you reach into your pocket (or purse) and take out a gift for your friend. With a smile, the old sage takes the gift and thanks you for it.

You turn and start down the side of the hill toward the meadow. You are aware of the smell of the forest and the sound of the birds in the trees. The sun feels good on your skin and you are singing a little song as you walk.

After doing the imagery, give yourself a little time and write down what you experienced.

FOR REFLECTION AND DISCUSSION

1. How did the exercise feel to you, overall?

2. Who was the sage? Man or woman? Did you know the person?

3. What advice did the old sage give to you about the suitcases? Write out what the sage said and how you felt as you listened.

4. What did the person give as a gift to you?

5. What did you give to the person?

6. How did you feel when you were going down the hill? Did you have the suitcases with you?

7. Are you going to do what the person said? Will you go back to see the person?

EXERCISE 4

THE STEPBACK:
FINDING THE SPACE TO
DISCOVER YOUR HEART

Diminished persons know only two methods of involvement: On the one hand, we persist. That is, we go
full speed ahead; we try harder and hold on tighter. Or, on
the other hand, we quit. We fold up and run away. There
is a time and place for both persisting and starting over,
for hanging in there and for pulling out. Most of the time,
however, what we need is something somewhere in between these two extremes. We need a method that gives
us the freedom to look at what we feel and what we think
in order to determine what we should do.

This exercise is one such tool. It is based on a dream I
had. In the dream, a young man who was a boxer came to
me for help in improving his fighting skills. He related to
me that he was losing all his fights and he did not know
what to do. He felt that he could do nothing to help himself. His opponents were overwhelming him as they hit
him repeatedly about the head and upper body.

"I think you should consider the stepback," I advised.
The "stepback," as I explained to him in the dream, is a
method by which he could remove himself from the fight
in order to understand what was happening to him.

"But isn't that running away?" he asked.

"No, it is giving yourself the necessary space and time to
look at who your opponent is and what he is doing to you
and how you feel about it all," I responded.

My dream ended at that point and I do not know what
happened to the young fighter. The stepback is without a
doubt poor boxing strategy. But, as I thought about it
later, it is a wonderfully therapeutic practice for the rest of

us. It enables us to remove ourselves from the heat of the moment in order to get at the underlying feelings rather than concentrate all our energies on the details of the situation and our thoughts about it.

So, let's do a stepback.

1. Write out a brief description of a specific event in your recent past (or a situation which you face today) which was painful for you or in some way felt overwhelming to you.

2. Now, imagine your inner child facing this same or a similar situation. Take a few minutes to "see" the child involved in the event. Imagine the child trying to solve your adult problem. Write out in the space below what the child sees.

List at least three things which the child felt in the situation.

1. _____

2. _____

3. _____

Describe briefly who or what the opponent was as the child perceived the situation.

What did the child *do* or want to do in the situation?

What were the skills that the child had to work with in dealing with the situation? Were there specific things which the child was missing that he or she needed to deal adequately with the situation?

3. What can you say to the child which will be of help to her or him?

4. How does this stepback help you with the problem you described in number one? Do you have greater understanding of yourself? The situation? The opponent you face? Your feelings? The things that are defeating you in the situation? Write out your responses to these questions.

FOR REFLECTION AND DISCUSSION

1. How did you feel as you were doing this exercise?

2. What important insights did you get about yourself as a
   result of doing the exercise?

3. Do you find that when you get into a stressful situation
   today, you revert to the painful feelings of that child
   and that you seem to have no more than the child's
   strengths to face your problems?

4. Consider this comment from Arthur, a middle-aged,
   successful businessman:
   "My problems look overwhelming to me because of
   the risks involved. I am afraid to fail but I know that
   to get to happiness we all have to risk unhappiness.
   But I can't risk failing and, therefore, I can't ever
   reach real joy. I don't believe I will ever be happy."

EXERCISE 5

IDENTIFYING AND FEELING FEELINGS

We diminished people have difficulty with our feelings in two very specific areas: We have trouble *identifying* feelings and we have trouble *expressing* feelings. Some of us have denied our feelings for so long and so effectively that we are unable to know what we feel. Some of us even say that we do not feel anything at all. And when we are able to identify a feeling, we are unable to let others know what that feeling is. It is as if we think that we are not worthy to have feelings like other people. Or, we fear that if we show our feelings, other people will not like or accept or approve of us. In short, if we feel, we won't be loved. This exercise is designed to help us learn how to identify our feelings and begin the process of expressing them.

First, let's look at healthy feelings. Normal people feel five feelings that we sometimes mislabel as negative emotions. They are:

Sadness
> When we do not get what we need, the normal feeling is sadness. As children, when we did not get hugged when we needed closeness, or when we were told that we were wrong or to shut up when we needed to talk, the natural emotional response was to be sad. We feel sadness when we do not get what we need as adults. Normal people can identify the feeling. They are aware of the pain and sometimes they may cry to express it.

Anger
> Not getting what we need or losing something special to us also produces anger. Our dysfunctional

family denied us the most necessary things for our proper development and then taught us to deny that we were angry about the loss. We were told that we were not supposed to be angry. Sometimes we use the words "frustration," "disgust," "irritation," or " being upset" when we are talking about our anger.

Fear

Fear is a sense that we are in danger. Something or someone threatens our well-being. We fear that we will die. The death may not be physical so much as emotional. We are anxious and have a feeling of foreboding and we believe that we will have to do something to protect ourselves but we do not know what to do.

Guilt

Guilt is the feeling that we have done something wrong. For children, it is the feeling that we have not lived up to our parents' expectations. Frequently for the diminished person, guilt comes from the same source. That is, we have not done what our parents expect and we feel guilt. This latter is neurotic guilt.

Shame

Shame is a frequent feeling of the child in a dysfunctional family. It is the feeling that we are bad, inferior, inadequate, or incompetent. We believe that there is something wrong with us. It is the same feeling as guilt. The difference is that guilt comes from *doing* something wrong while shame comes from *being* something wrong.

Now, let's see how we felt and expressed these feelings during childhood and how we experience them today as an adult. Pick one of the above feelings that seems to have been a problem for you as a child and may be a problem for you as an adult. If you have trouble remembering your feelings from childhood or knowing your feelings as an adult, pick the feeling that seems most interesting to you. After selecting one of the emotions answer each of the following with reference to that emotion.

1. The feeling that I select is _____.

2. The following are three reasons why it is important for me to deal with this feeling:

   _____

   _____

   _____

   _____

3. The following are four experiences in my childhood when I felt _____. (If you can't remember your feelings in childhood, select four times when you *could* have felt the feeling you have chosen.)

   _____

   _____

   _____

   _____

   _____

4. Which of the following did you do with this feeling when you were a child or adolescent?
   ☐ Acted like I was not feeling it.
   ☐ Cried.
   ☐ Expressed it in an open and proper fashion.
   ☐ Stuffed it back into my heart and denied it.

☐ Ate food to cover it up.
☐ Tried harder to please.
☐ Hid or ran away.
☐ Was sarcastic or pouted.
☐ Prayed harder to be a better person.
☐ Told someone about my feeling.
☐ Other (describe).

5. If you told someone about your feelings, who was it and how did they respond?

6. Please answer the following about your parents:

My Mother: (Check the most appropriate answers.)
☐ Never noticed my feelings.
☐ Noticed and made me feel better.
☐ Noticed and made me feel worse.
☐ Required me to stop feeling my feelings.
☐ Encouraged me to talk about how I was feeling.
☐ Embarrassed and shamed me about my feelings.
☐ Other (describe).

My Father:
☐ Never noticed my feelings.
☐ Noticed and made me feel better.
☐ Noticed and made me feel worse.
☐ Required me to stop feeling my feelings.
☐ Encouraged me to talk about how I was feeling.
☐ Embarrassed and shamed me about my feelings.
☐ Other (describe).

7. Draw a picture of the feeling you have chosen as you felt it when you were a child or adolescent. This picture is an illustration of how you felt when you were a child. If you wish, the picture can be no more than a group of stick figures or you may wish to cut a cartoon or a picture from the newspaper which captures how you felt. If you have trouble remembering your feelings from childhood, draw how you think you *should* have felt if you had been allowed to be what you were.

8. Now draw a picture of the chosen feeling as you experience it as an adult.

FOR REFLECTION AND DISCUSSION

1. What feelings came up for you when you were describing your father and mother in the exercise?

2. What insights do you get into yourself when you compare the picture you drew in response to #7 with that in #8?

3. How do you see feelings expressed in the healthy people and healthy families you know?

4. How are emotions expressed in your family today? At your church? On the job?

5. Do you participate in any groups today which encourage the healthy expression of all feelings? If not, what groups are available to you?

EXERCISE 6

FEELING FEELINGS AND FAMILY DENIAL

Diminished persons grow up in families where feelings get *minimized* ("That's nothing, you should see how I feel"), discounted ("You shouldn't feel that way"), or *rationalized* ("Here is what you need to do to take care of that problem"). This exercise is designed to help you identify ways in which you learned to disqualify the reality of your emotions in your family and how you continue to practice the same dysfunctional patterns as an adult.

Write out an experience from your childhood or adolescent years in which you remember having experienced strong emotions. Give the details of the experience not only about what happened but what you felt as you remember it. Think in terms of specific emotions like sadness, anger, fear, guilt, shame, joy, pride, satisfaction, or love. Do not use emotional euphemisms like "I was upset," or "I was frustrated."

When my family found out about this
experience, they responded to it by _____
_____
_____
_____
_____
_____

Or, my family never found out about my feelings because:

I pretended to feel _____

_____

_____

In reality I felt _____

_____

_____

Today as an adult, I still tend to minimize, discount, or disqualify my feelings in the following ways:

1. _____

_____

_____

2. _____

_____

_____

3. _____

_____

_____

4. _____

_____

_____

FOR REFLECTION AND DISCUSSION

This exercise is designed to help us recognize situations in the present where we discount and minimize our feelings. Hopefully we will learn to be more transparent to ourselves and thus more skilled at identifying and expressing our feelings and needs. As we do, the likelihood increases that our needs will be met. We also multiply our potential for intimacy with others and we also become more comfortable with ourselves and like ourselves much more.

1. How did you feel as you did this exercise?

2. What are some of the ways you can use to help you identify clearly what you are feeling?

3. How can you begin to express your feelings more directly to people that are appropriate for them?

4. How can you begin to distinguish between safe and unsafe people?

EXERCISE 7

GRIEVING AND LEAVING THE PAST

Diminished people have a lot of things to grieve. Yet, because we have spent so much time covering up and smoothing over our feelings, we are not very good at grief. So, we have to learn to grieve. We have been doing exercises which force us into the past and make us look at what we lost and how we were hurt by the experiences of our lives. There were a number of things which we needed as a child and did not get. We still need them and we are still not getting them. These are real losses and, just as when we lose someone to death, we must deal with the grief involved.

Healthy children learn:
- Life is okay.
- I am okay.
- I can discover my needs.
- I can have wants and have them met.
- Change is possible.
- I can have a positive effect on my world.
- There are shades of grey, not just black and white.
- Problems can be discussed.
- Other people are there for my support and I am there for theirs.
- Criticism will not kill me.
- I can confront others without destroying them or being destroyed by them.

Diminished children do not learn these things. Instead, we learn:
- Life is to be gotten through because it hurts.

- If I were okay, my parents would not have so many problems.
- I can have neither wants nor wishes.
- Change is too hard even to think about.
- Everything is either black or white.
- Problems are to be ignored through compulsive behavior.
- If I confront someone, he will be deeply hurt (destroyed) and he won't love me anymore.
- Something is wrong with me.

In order to recover and to return to wholeness, we must grieve the losses of our childhood. Our first grief is the loss of our childhood. Instead of a healthy childhood that brought us wholeness and growth, we were diminished. Unfortunately, we are given only one set of childhood years. Ours was not pretty and we will never have another. That is a loss that we must face and grieve.

Our second deprivation to be grieved is unconditional parental love. We were never loved unconditionally by our parents and we will never get unconditional love from our parents. Part of our problem as adults is that we have never faced the loss of that unconditional love and we still are trying to get it. Grieving it helps us give it up.

The third grief we must experience is the pain of the shaming events we had while growing up. We have worked hard to keep those experiences buried deep in our unconscious. Now we must dig them up and go through the pain of feeling the feelings we have sought to avoid.

The fourth loss that diminished persons must grieve is the loss of the compulsions we developed to get through life without feelings. We must surrender the habits which we have used to avoid the pain.

The fifth deprivation that we must grieve is the loss of the role that we took on to survive in our chaotic family.

We were necessary in our family because we were the hero or the scapegoat. Or, maybe we made them all laugh and forget their pain. We placated, or served, or succeeded in order to take care of them in the hope that they would love us. Now we must give up this self-defeating role. And we are afraid to give up the role because, self-destructive and painful as it is, this role has always given us meaning. But when we begin to recover, that role stops working.

Grief then is a prerequisite to healing. In fact, in its first stages, the process of recovery is the process of grief. As long as we hold on to the old ways (that is, refuse to have the experience of loss), we will not begin the healing process of recovery.

SO . . . FOLLOW THE CIRCLE OF HEALING

1. Acknowledge the *denial* that hides the hurt.

2. Acknowledge the *hurt* that hides the loss and loneliness.

3. Acknowledge the *loss and loneliness* that hides the lack of self-worth.

4. Acknowledge the *lack of self-worth* that hides the anger.

5. Acknowledge the *anger* that hides the denial.

6. Begin at number one again.

FOR REFLECTION AND DISCUSSION

1. This exercise is designed to cause you to think about how you do, or do not, express your grief. What part of the exercise most caught your attention? Why do you suppose that part was of most interest to you?

2. How do you hide the grief about your losses? What emotions are you trying to deny by hiding your grief?

3. In what specific ways has thinking about your grief helped you to deal with your losses?

4. Consider the following comment made by Karen, a forty-four year old divorcee:

   For years I excused my father and protected him by thinking that I really didn't have much to complain about. After all, he never beat me. He just never said, "I love you," and he never put his arms around me. But now I know that I was hurt just as much as if he had hit me physically.

   What does Karen have to grieve? What do you think she can do to handle the grief? How would you, if you were in her situation?

Part Two

SEEING YOURSELF
AS YOU
REALLY ARE

The legacy of the past is that we diminished persons never have a clear perception of who we are. There are so many good qualities about us that we completely miss. We have strengths that we hardly know and never really enjoy. To paraphrase the old song, we accentuate the negative and forget the positive in our lives. We expect the worse and then confirm our prophesies by looking for the bad things as we disregard the good. Why do we do that and how can we stop? These are the questions that are at the heart of the next six exercises. How can we overcome the past and begin to see ourselves as we really can become?

EXERCISE 8

SHAME vs GUILT

Diminished people often mistake the emotions of shame and guilt for one another. We do so for two reasons: 1) We are not good with emotions and 2) the two emotions are in some ways so similar. We frequently give the name guilt to what is more properly called shame and for that reason often have difficulty dealing with either emotion. This exercise is designed to help us distinguish between the two and to deal with each in a healthy fashion.

I. Differentiating Guilt and Shame

Guilt is about what we *do* and shame is about what we *are*. When we fail to act according to certain expectations, the emotion we experience is guilt. Guilt is a useful emotion when treated in a healthy manner. It is designed to make us aware when we have stepped over proper boundaries and to remind us that we need to change our ways.

Guilt is healthy when:
1. The expectations we have failed to meet are at the conscious level.
2. The expectations belong to us in the present and not to someone from our past.
3. The expectations are healthy and contribute to our overall well-being.
4. The guilt is not over two weeks old.

Shame, on the other hand, comes from our secrets. That is, our shame is about all those things we feel that we must hide from other people if we are to have their respect, approval, and love. So, anything we think we must keep hidden or that we must lie about is our shame. Shame is *never* healthy and is very hard to deal with because we frequently deny what we are shamed about.

II. What to do about guilt.

Healthy guilt is a very easy emotion to deal with. When we become aware that we have not lived up to a healthy rule that we agree with and want in our life, we can ask the following questions:

1. Am I personally responsible for breaking the rule? That is, did I do it deliberately and with foreknowledge? If the answer to this question is *No,* the guilt is unhealthy and we may forget it. If the answer is *Yes,* we may proceed to the next question.
2. Is there something I can do about it? Again, if the answer is *No,* forget the guilt. If it is *Yes,* go on.
3. Do I want to do it? If our response to this question is *No,* we may forget the guilt. If, however, our answer is *Yes,* we may proceed to number four.
4. Do it and we may forget the guilt.
5. Remember that guilt that is old is leftover guilt and probably comes from expectations of someone else. It is neurotic guilt and is unhealthy. We can throw it away like we would moldy leftovers in our refrigerator. *Most of the time unhealthy guilt is SHAME.*

III. What to do about our shame.

Shame cannot bear the light of day. It exists only when it can remain hidden. Therefore, anything we do to share our shame with another person or to get it out into the clear light of our own consciousness is in itself a therapeutic act. Shame recedes before self-acceptance and openness in safe places in the same way that darkness recedes in the presence of the light.

To deal with shame.
1. Identify your *shame areas* from the past. What are the things about yourself that you hope other people won't notice or find out about? What subjects do you dread coming up in conversation with friends or family? What are the things about your past which you cannot accept about yourself?
2. Identify *shame events*. What are the events that embarrass or trouble you most when you think about doing them today? Are there occurrences or certain kinds of events that you try especially hard to avoid?
3. Identify *shame parts* of your body. What physical aspects of your body do you hate for others to become aware of? Are there specific ways you dress in order to shield part of your physique from others' awareness? How do you regard the signs of your physical aging?
4. Identify *shame thoughts*. Are there particular thoughts that you would be ashamed of if others knew you were thinking them?
5. Identify *shame behaviors and expectations*. What behaviors do you engage in that you would hate for

others to know about? Do you have opinions or evaluations of yourself that you cannot tell to other people around you?

6. Make a list of the things you have identified under each of the above categories. Find a safe person or group and share the entire list one topic at a time with this person or group. Do not leave anything out. Tell it in detail.

7. Develop a relationship with one person or one small group in which secrets are unnecessary. Be aware that this relationship is functional to the extent that you may be free to tell it all. It is a relationship in which there is no shame and therefore a relationship which will facilitate health and growth.

FOR REFLECTION AND DISCUSSION

1. How do you confuse guilt and shame? How does this confusion lead to troubles in dealing with these two emotions?

2. Using the distinctions in shame and guilt made in this exercise, which do you think you experience more, guilt or shame? What are those things about which you feel guilty? Which things do you feel shame about?

3. Consider the following comment from Barbara, a thirty-seven year old school teacher and mother of two. How can her statement be of help to you?
   "I have no time for destructive thinking, pessimistic self-talk, or beliefs that hinder my recovery. So I throw out the emotions of guilt and and shame. I am not guilty and I have no reason to feel shame. I discard these limiting emotions like moldy bread stored too long on the backside of my kitchen cabinets."

EXERCISE 9

GETTING UNDER YOUR SKIN:
FINDING THE WHOLES IN THE INNER YOU

1. Please list three things about which you feel most guilty. (These may be recent things or they may be from the past.)

    1.

    2.

    3.

2. Select one of the above and answer the following questions:

    1. What is the specific rule which you have failed to keep?

    2. Is there something concrete which you may do about the situation or the people involved? If so, what?

    3. Are you willing to do that? ☐ Yes ☐ No

    4. If yes, what keeps you from doing it?

3. What are some of the things which you think other people generally find unacceptable or unlikable about you?

4. When viewing yourself in a full-length mirror, what part of your body do you look at first? Which part most often?

5. What thoughts go through your head that you fight hard to control and keep out and that you are afraid other people might discover?

6. What kind of events and/or interactions do you generally wish to avoid?

7. Imagine yourself being introduced to a person with whom you think you may want to be friends. What are the things about you which you dread this person finding out? In other words, what about you do you expect this person to find objectionable? What strategies do you plan to use to keep these traits from his or her knowledge?

FOR REFLECTION AND DISCUSSION

1. What specific things did you learn about yourself from doing this exercise?

2. With reference to guilt and shame, where do you have the most work to do in your life? What specific things do you plan to do to deal with your guilt? Your shame?

3. Do you have a lot of "old" or "neurotic" guilt in your life? If you do, what do you plan to do to rid yourself of this destructive guilt?

4. Do you have a lot of guilt that is based on rules which are not yours? If you do, what can you do to remove this kind of guilt?

5. How has this exercise helped you to understand the shame in your life?

6. Following the suggestions in Exercise 8, who is a safe person with whom you can share your feelings of shame in order to get rid of them?

EXERCISE 10

OVERCOMING SHAME:
LEARNING TO LOVE THE INNER YOU

All feelings and thoughts about your value and worth are embodied in the outer you. For the co-dependent, they are based on shame and are so distorted and inaccurate that they may be called a false image of the Self. Yet they seem so real that you think that this  outer self is what you really are. The figure to the right portrays the relationship of the inner and outer self.

This outer shell is full of mistaken feelings and inaccurate information about the Self. Yet it functions to wall off that true inner reality. The more firmly fixed these feelings and beliefs, the more inflexible are the ideas, the more rigid and impenetrable the wall.

In your shame, you reason that the wall serves to "protect" the Self, to keep it from the rejection, abandonment, and death you fear. But it also limits and stunts the Self. You are limited in your expressions and your life is less rich and meaningful. You have less productivity and less joy and love. Rather than feeling protected and safe, you are actually afraid of life. And, what is worse, you may live your entire life without ever realizing how vast is the inner potential that lies there walled off from view.

How does one break past this wall of shame and fear? Let me make five suggestions:

1. Do the things that are too painful to do. Become

vulnerable and take risks. Break some of your unbreakable rules.

Make a list of three of your rules that have been important in guiding behavior that you intend to break.

2. Find a safe person and/or group and share your secrets. Some people use a spiritual director for this purpose. Others join a twelve-step program. So long as it is safe, who the audience is does not matter. What works is the process.

List the safe people and the safe groups in your life. If you do not have more than two persons and one group, write out your plan to find more.

3. Open yourself up to God, as you understand him. At bottom, this whole process is spiritual.

Write out your concept of God and the place of spiritual things in your life. How can these realities become more personally real to you?

4. Find silence and enter that inner cavern. Prayer, meditation, imagery — these are all avenues to link you to the inner self.

How do you relate to silence? Do you have a time each day in which you draw into yourself and find the inner quiet? How can this become more effective in your personal growth?

5. Place *value* on that inner self. Love the child. Become aware of the way in which you chose the illusions of the outer self. Look for ways to honor the value of that true self.

List three sentences that are part of your critical self-talk. Do these sentences sound like significant others from your growing-up years? In other words, are you critical of yourself like adults were when you were a child? Self-acceptance and self-valuing comes when we begin to silence that inner self-critical voice.

FOR REFLECTION AND DISCUSSION

1. What are the parts of this exercise which most caught your attention? How do you feel about the practical suggestions made for dealing with shame? Are there suggestions that seem especially useful to you?
2. Contemplate the wisdom of this ancient poem from India:

> *Oh, let the self exalt itself,*
> *Not sink itself below:*
> *Self is the only friend of self,*
> *And self Self's only foe.*
> *For self, when it subdues itself,*
> *Befriends itself. And so*
> *When it eludes self-conquest, is*
> *Its own and only foe.*
>
> *So calm, so self-subdued, the Self*
> *Has an unshaken base*
> *Through pain and pleasure, cold and heat,*
> *Through honor and disgrace.*

What does this poem mean to you?
3. Consider the following Peanuts cartoon. How is Olaf following the suggestions of this exercise? Do you still compete at "Ugly Dog Contests"?

 Peanuts   BY CHARLES M. SCHULZ

Reprinted with permission of UFS, Inc.

EXERCISE 11

POSITIVE PERSONS

Even in the life of the most diminished person there are usually at least a few positive persons. That is, there are people for whom we had respect and who we thought we would like to grow up to be like. We may have known these individuals personally and they may have had a direct impact on our lives. Or, we may have only read about them and known them only in our thoughts and imagination. Even so, they have made an impact on who or what we grew up to be. In fact, some of them may be alive in us today and for that reason we need to go back and think about them. Please answer the following questions about your childhood and teenage years. Try to be specific and detailed in your answers.

1. Who is the person you admired most when you were growing up? (write in name) _____.

2. What exactly are the characteristics you admired about this person?

3. Please describe your favorite experience with this person. (Use extra paper, if necessary.)

4. What are the things this person has taught you (by example or word) which have made a difference in your life?

5. What do you wish you could do for or say to this person today?

6. What one thing do you wish you could hear this person say to you today?

FOR REFLECTION AND DISCUSSION

1. Share with at least one person your answers to the questions in this exercise. How does it feel to talk about your positive person?

2. What, if any, new insights into yourself did this exercise give to you?

3. What characteristics of this person do you see in yourself? What can you do to develop in yourself more of the qualities which you admired in this person?

4. What things keep you from being more like this person?

EXERCISE 12

MEETING WITH YOUR POSITIVE FRIEND

In the previous exercise, you described an uncommon individual in your life, a person from your past who has influenced you in a positive manner. At least a couple of times in the next few days, I want you to imagine meeting with your friend in a special way. Be open to what happens as you think through this exercise. Do not weigh yourself down with negative expectations. Let new and creative thoughts come as a gift to you. Follow these suggestions and feel free to add to them in any way that makes this exercise more comfortable for you.

Imagine your friend waiting for you in some quiet place where you have met before. Let the surroundings be peaceful and joyful for you and your friend. Take some time to be present at that scene. Be aware of how it feels to be there and what thoughts being there brings out in you.

Let your friend praise you for the things he or she sees in you.

Don't resist or protest.

Be silent and do not try to think of what you will say to your friend to pay back the compliments.

Listen and enjoy.

Ask your friend, "What is my greatest strength, in your estimation?"

Be silent and listen. Believe what your friend says.

Take time to reflect on the ways that your friend has influenced your life in positive ways.

Take a moment to tell your friend what he or she has meant to you. Thank him or her for being in your life. Leave the place thanking your friend for meeting you there and asking that you might meet again.

After a brief time write down what transpired during the visit.

FOR REFLECTION AND DISCUSSION

1. How did you feel as you did this imagery? If you did it more than once, was it different from one time to the next? In what ways?

2. Consider again how you are like this person? In what ways are you different? What are those qualities which your friend has which you wish you had?

3. What keeps you from being more like your positive friend? How may you grow to be more of the positive things which your friend is?

4. The Plains Indians of North America believed that any idea, object, or person could be a Medicine Wheel to us by serving as a mirror in which we see our own reflection. They felt that we meet ourselves in everything we confront. How may this positive person whom you have described and with whom you have now spent this time serve as a mirror in which you see your reflection? In what ways is that thought a "Medicine Wheel" for you?

EXERCISE 13

LEARNING TO:

ACCEPT COMPLIMENTS,
EVALUATE CRITICISM,
EMBRACE SUCCESS,
AND ADMIT FAILURE
WITHOUT LOSING YOURSELF

Compliments in a healthy family are true statements about the positive qualities of the child. These compliments are about the value of the child and the parents' awareness of and love for what the child is. On the other hand, compliments in an unhealthy family are manipulative tools. In the healthy family, children learn to accept and believe compliments while we diminished children have a hard time trusting the compliments and grow up not being able to accept them.

Criticism, however, is a different matter. The child from the dysfunctional family cannot trust a compliment but we seem to welcome criticism, automatically accepting it as valid and deserved. We are closed to compliments but are open to criticism. We accept criticism because we believe we deserve it. Thus we feel we can trust the criticism but the compliment is not warranted and therefore we are uncomfortable with it.

Further, success in dysfunctional families is usually defined by our parents. It almost always is what they define as success and therefore involves a bundle of "shoulds." Living in that atmosphere takes all the joy out of accomplishments because one has only done what one "should" based on the expectations of another. Where is the satisfaction in that? Usually we ask in this context, "What is

the next thing I must accomplish?'' Life becomes but a
series of never-ending hurdles that one must continually
leap. We may accomplish a great deal (jump many hurdles), but we never feel like a success. We are never happy
or satisfied with what we have accomplished. For us there
are no successes because our successes are never enough.
No matter what we accomplish, we always feel like fail-
ures.

So, diminished children grow up to be diminished a-
dults who can't accept compliments, who seek criticism,
and who always carry with them the feeling that they have
failed even when they have succeeded in the goals they
have sought. Our mind-set becomes, ''Whatever I do is
not enough.''

This exercise is designed to help us begin to trust and
accept compliments, evaluate criticism before accepting
it as valid, redefine success for ourselves, and admit only
legitimate failure.

1. Go back into your childhood and adolescence and
remember the compliments you received. As you do, for-
mulate answers to the following questions.

What kind of things did people compliment you for?

_____

_____

_____

_____

_____

Who complimented you?   _____

Who did not compliment you? _____

What were your feelings and thoughts when you were complimented? _____

_____

_____

_____

2. To be judged a success as a child I had to _____

_____

_____

_____

_____

Success for me today is   _____

_____

_____

Make a list of the greatest accomplishments you have made in your life. After each one describe how much joy the accomplishment gave you.

Make a list of the "shoulds" which are at the basis of your definition of success.

Describe how your successes are "never enough." Include in your answer how each success is immediately followed by involvement in another undertaking?

FOR REFLECTION AND DISCUSSION

1. What did this exercise mean to you? What part of it most caught your attention?

2. Suggestions for you to consider:
   1. Compliments:
      When you are complimented, pause for a moment and then simply say, "Thank you." Then pause again before continuing the conversation. *Say nothing about the compliment and do not return it.*
   2. Criticism:
      • Hear it. Evaluate its validity. Assess how you may use it.
      • Realize that it is your behavior and not you that is being evaluated.
      • Take time to think about the criticism.
      • Become responsible for your own needs. Being self-critical often comes from not liking yourself.
      • Address the issues that allow you to feel better about yourself. If a criticism is valid, do what you can to fix it. If it is not, ask for what you need and/or do what is necessary to have that recognized.
   3. Successes:
      • Learn to enjoy your successes.
      • Set your own goals. Kick out others' "shoulds."
      • Be aware of your accomplishments.
      • Know your own needs and wants and the difference between the two.
      • Let your behavior be guided by *your* needs.
      • Say *"NO."* Enjoy it.

- Ask "why should I?" "Is this my goal or someone else's?" Allow your behavior to be based on what you genuinely want for yourself. This requires self-honesty, thinking, and the ability to say "No." Helpful questions are, "Why should I?" "Who says so?" and "Do I really want to?"

4. Failure:
   - Remember that failure is a part of all human lives. Give yourself permission to be a part of the human race by failing from time to time.
   - Differentiate between *self* and your *behaviors* or *actions.* Thus, when failure occurs, think of it as an act or event or project failing, not as you failing. Say, "My plans for the project failed," not "I failed in pulling the project off."

5. How do you relate to this statement made by Linda, a forty-two year old nurse:
   "I feel that I must always be better than, in order to be good enough."

Part Three

TAKING CONTROL OF YOUR LIFE

This section contains eight exercises that encourage us to look at some of the core issues of the diminished person's life. These matters are at the core because their pain has been with us so long and because they are so much a part of us. In fact, just as the cripple lets go of his crutches only with the greatest reluctance, so we may have trouble imagining life without them.

These core issues are associated both with things we do as well as things we fail to do. These are issues which are left from our diminished past and which we continue to practice into our adulthood. They have to do with games we play, roles we fill, rules we follow, expectations we have, where we want to go, how we define ourselves, and what we fear. These issues are about what controls us and how we can take that power back. The question of this section is: How can we be in charge of our own lives?

EXERCISE 14

DEFENSIVE POSTURING
or
Relearning the Destructive Survival
Tactics We Learned as a Child

Part of the task of the growing-up years is to learn to cope with and survive unpleasant things that we encounter along the way. Life never gives us exactly what we want and we have to learn to deal with negative things. In unwholesome social surroundings, including family settings, what we learn is coping mechanisms which help us survive the trauma of our environment but are themselves unhealthy and self-destructive. Unfortunately, when we grow into adults, we continue to practice these dysfunctional survival tactics even though we no longer need them. They were necessary for us to cope with our traumatic surroundings as children but they hamper our life as an adult. This exercise is designed to help us identify our negative and dysfunctional defensive postures and learn more effective and healthy ways of dealing with our environment.

NEGATIVE DEFENSIVE POSTURES

1) Frozen feelings. Frozen feelings means discounting our feelings and not being able to know what we are feeling or not being able to express what we do feel. Being "nice," "polite," "tactful," and pretending to feel things that we do not feel and not to feel the things we do feel are examples of frozen feelings. This defense is all about denial. We learn especially to deny the negative and vulnerable feelings like anxiety, fear, loneliness, grief, rejection, needing, and caring. Concomitant with denial is the rule, never ask for help or tell others what is going on.

Childhood Survival Value: Keeps us from taking responsibility for our feelings and makes us feel less vulnerable.

2) Control. This defense means that we must be in control of all our feelings and behavior as well as the behavior of others. We get anxious when we are not in control of the world, including the thoughts, feelings, and behavior of others. This factor includes the need to make a perfect world for everybody.

Childhood Survival Value: Keeps us from feeling vulnerable and helps us to overcome the fear of abandonment by giving us the illusion of our necessity to others.

3) Perfectionism. Perfectionism is based on the belief that anything less than perfect means failure. Diminished people will do anything to avoid the feeling of failure. The demand of perfectionism is that we always be "right." We learn to do the right thing and never be responsible for any wrong thing.

Childhood Survival Value: Makes us seem somehow more necessary in our family and therefore less likely to be abandoned. Perfectionism also helps us combat our growing sense of worthlessness by making us feel that we are good.

4) Dishonesty. Dishonesty means more than that we tell lies. It also means that we hide our true feelings, perceptions, thoughts, and reality. Dishonesty means that we do not tell the truth. Sometimes we are so deep in our own denial that we do not know what the truth is and thus are dishonest with ourselves. When this happens, we resort to

telling what we think the other person wants or needs to hear. Dishonesty makes us keep personal and family secrets.

Childhood Survival Value: Protects our weak ego and keeps us from rejection.

5) Thinking disorders. When we come from a traumatic family, we usually develop a confused and obsessive thinking pattern that is similar to the unrealistic thinking characteristic of the entire family system.

Childhood Survival Value: Disordered thinking helps us make "sense" of the chaotic world in which we live. It becomes a "filter" through which reality is strained and as such protects us from the dissonance which would result from knowing that what our parents defined as real was not in fact objective reality. Though painful, we continue to hold on to the dysfunctional and contorted definitions of truth.

GROWTH-RELATED DEFENSES

1) I will share my problems and express my persistent feelings to the appropriate person in an effort to get feedback about myself from others about what is really going on. I will begin to speak for myself directly to whomever is appropriate for the message.

Make a list of the persons with whom you will begin to share the truth about yourself.

2) I will develop methods of getting to know and respect myself. I will learn to do things for me and know that caring for myself is healthy.

Make a list of the methods you will use to get to know you.

3) I will become aware of my need for perfection and will begin the process of giving up the need to be right all the time. I will know that the pain I feel in surrendering the perfectionism is the pain I have always tried to avoid.

What rules of perfectionism will you deliberately break?

4) I will learn and start to practice the Serenity Prayer. I will forgive myself when I fail!

Obtain a copy of the Serenity Prayer (if you do not already know it) and write it in here.

5) I will let myself have fun, even be silly sometimes.

Make a list of the things which you like to do merely because they are fun.

6) I will learn that conflict is often not about me and I will learn to face conflict without fear.

Make a list of the rules which have guided your behavior as far as conflict is concerned and how you are going to change these rules so as to make them more healthy.

7) I will love me unconditionally.

If you do, what will you do differently?

8) I will follow through with actions, not just words.

Make a list of areas in which you intend to replace words with action.

FOR REFLECTION AND DISCUSSION

1. What stuck out for you in this exercise? How did it make you feel about yourself? About your past? Your future?

2. Go back and look at the childhood survival values of the negative defense postures. Which of these seem most appropriate for your childhood? Are they still a part of your life today?

3. How does developing more growth-related defenses help you reduce your need for these childhood holdovers?

4. Consider the behavior of the person in this cartoon. How is her behavior a negative defense? Do you ever do what she is doing?

ADAM
Copyright 1989 Universal Press Syndicate
Reprinted with permission. All rights reserved.

EXERCISE 15

ANGER IS A HAPPY
(*and useful*) EMOTION

We talk about "getting rid of anger," or "doing something with anger," as if it were a stigma or something to be ashamed of. It is almost as if we are *bad* if we are *mad*. We seem to fear our anger and think of it as an unworthy emotion that we should never feel. Or, if we do, we are to get rid of it as soon as we can. We believe that it will destroy us if we do not.

What I would like for you to think about doing instead of getting rid of your anger is transforming yourself by using your anger. When you do, you allow your anger to become that for which it was intended.

Consider this exchange between Martha and George, a couple who have been married twenty-two years:

MARTHA: (lying in bed reading a book) Every time I read a book on marriage enrichment, I think that there is so much more that we could have in our marriage.
GEORGE: (turning his back to Martha) Then quit reading those books.

Step One: UNDERSTANDING ANGER
When you are devalued as a person, the emotion which you feel is anger. Anything which effectively blocks you from the objectives of life that are yours by right produces anger. These things may be spontaneous occurrences that life brings to you. Or, they may be conscious or unconscious deeds done by others or even by yourself. But when you are thwarted in the natural fulfillment of your needs as a human being, the emotion that results is *always* anger.

In the example above, what are three needs which Martha is being denied?

1.

2.

3.

Step Two: ACCEPTING ANGER

The purpose of anger is self-protection. Our anger alerts us to things in our environment that can be damaging to our value as a person. Anger says, "Hey, watch out. Something is there which can destroy your personhood. Be ready."

How do George's words reveal an attitude which can be destructive to Martha?

Step Three: USING ANGER

Properly understood and properly accepted, your anger is an energizing emotion. It can mobilize you to take action like Jesus did in throwing the money-changing scoundrels out of God's temple. Anger is a wonderful emotion because it says, "I am too valuable for this to happen to me. You cannot continue to devalue me because I will not allow it."

Put to this kind of use, anger becomes an expression of *love*; love for self, love for others, love for God and his creation. Rather than a shameful emotion which we must hide, it becomes the creative and protective emotion which God intended it to be.

There are at least two healthy uses of anger:

1) Feeling the feeling and acting angrily. Feeling anger and acting angrily are not always the same, but sometimes acting out our anger can be a healthy thing to do.

What do you think would be a healthy way for Martha to act out her anger toward George?

2. Feeling the feeling and affirming yourself. Self-affirmation means to ask directly for what you need and then move to begin the process to get it.

What are three things that Martha could do to affirm her needs in this relationship?

1.

2.

3.

CONCLUSION

After doing this exercise, can you see how Martha's anger can transform her and give her greater control of her life? How can you begin to use your anger to transform you?

FOR REFLECTION AND DISCUSSION

1. What needs in your life are not being met and what do you do with your anger about it?

2. How was anger handled in your house when you were a child? How have you imitated those methods of dealing with anger in your life?

3. Consider the following list of myths about anger. Which of the myths of anger is most a part of your beliefs?

MYTHS ABOUT ANGER AND THE BELIEFS THAT SUSTAIN THEM

ANGER IS A NEGATIVE EMOTION
- Nice people don't get angry.
- I'm not okay when I feel anger.
- Anger is a waste of time and energy.
- Anger is a sinful emotion.

ANGER DESTROYS RELATIONSHIPS
- I will lose control and say things I'll regret if I get angry.
- People will leave me if I get angry at them.
- If I feel angry at someone, the relationship is over and that person must go away.
- If someone gets angry at me, they will leave me.

IF I FEEL ANGER, SOMETHING IS WRONG
- If someone gets angry at me, it is because I have done something wrong.
- If someone gets angry at me, I am responsible and must fix them.

ANGER AND VIOLENCE ARE THE SAME
- If I feel angry at someone, I must punish that person for making me feel angry.
- If I feel angry at someone, that person has to change what he or she is doing so I don't feel angry any more.
- If I feel angry, I must hit someone or break something.
- If I feel angry, someone will hit me and abandon me.

ANGER AND LOVE ARE MUTUALLY EXCLUSIVE
- If I feel angry at someone, it means I don't love that person anymore.
- If someone feels angry at me, it means that person doesn't love me anymore.
- It is a truly terrible thing for someone to be angry at me.

I MUST JUSTIFY MY ANGER WITH A
REASONABLE EXPLANATION
- It's okay to feel angry only when I have a reasonable explanation for my feelings.

4. What keeps you from using your anger as a self-empowering emotion?

EXERCISE 16

PLAYING THE GAME BY
SOMEBODY ELSE'S RULES

Children entering an unhealthy family system must figure out how they can adapt to the mess. Everybody is trying to survive in the midst of a set of relationships that is out of balance and unwholesome. In such a family, the child's needs are never met, especially the needs for security, love, and acceptance. The child seldom has the feeling "I belong here," "I am safe," or "There is someone for me." Rather, the child learns a body of rules.

The purpose of all rules, healthy or otherwise, is to maintain the status quo. They keep the family in balance. The most powerful are those that are not written down or transmitted verbally. These rules are not explicit. No one ever says, as an example, "In this family you do not talk about money." Or, there is not a bulletin board on which is written, "In this family no one is allowed to question God's commandments. *THIS MEANS YOU.*" Everyone simply knows what the taboo subjects are. The child learns the rules and obeys them unquestioningly. Most of the time, we follow the rules without even being consciously aware of them.

As an example, my mother used to say when I was a child, "If you try hard enough, everybody will like you." Under the surface of this well-meaning statement is the iron-clad rule, "You must get everyone you meet to like you." I struggled with that one through childhood and adolescence. But my problems really started with that unwritten, unconscious rule when I became a man and went out to make a living. For two decades, I measured myself against an impossible and inhuman standard dictated by an inward precept of which I was unaware: Everyone must like me.

The purpose of this exercise is two-fold: 1) To help you become consciously aware of the rules that you learned as a child and continue blindly to follow as an adult and 2) to give you the opportunity to re-write the rule or to throw it out if you so chose.

1. Write out in the space below any sayings or myths that your family had. The following are examples that may get you started:

"You can't get too much education."
"Never trust anybody."
"Hard work never hurt anybody."
"Don't question authority."
"Don't talk, don't feel, and don't share."
"Try harder."
"Ignore it and it will go away."
"Don't lose control; be strong."
"Feel guilty if you break the rules."
"Don't grow up/Grow up."

2. Consider carefully how you and your family translated these sayings into rules. Write out the rules that you see coming from these sayings.

3. Add to the list in #2 any other rules which your family advocated. Do not leave out religious ideas and customs as a source of rules.

4. You now have a lengthy list of family rules that you learned as a child. Rearrange them into two lists on another sheet of paper. The first list will be healthy rules which you want to keep. The second will be a list of rules which you want either to change into more healthy concepts or to throw out of your life.

Keep the following in mind to help you distinguish the healthy from unhealthy rules:

Healthy rules tend to be humane. That is, it is possible for human beings to follow them and they may be done in a human way. Unhealthy rules, on the other hand, are inhumane. They are double binds from the start because they cannot be done by humans. For example, take the well-known rule, "Children should be seen and not heard." How many two-year olds do you know who can live up to that one?

Healthy rules are flexible. They may, as an example, be different for different people. Unhealthy rules, to the contrary, are rigid. They say, "Everyone in this family does . . ." No allowance is made for individual differences. Consistent but flexible rules in a healthy system also mean that the person matters more than the rule.

Rules in a healthy atmosphere encourage openness. People want to share, to talk, to communicate. The statement, "You are as sick as your secrets," is true. Unhealthy rules, contrariwise, encourage denial, manipulation, and deceit. Secrets are very important in an atmosphere of unhealthy rules.

Healthy rules validate everyone's self-worth. The rules are not used to put down a person. No one is made to feel unworthy. Everyone has a value; if you are not good at sports, you can be good at writing.

In a healthy rule, there is unconditional acceptance of the person. Unhealthy rules, however, provide only for conditional acceptance. Each person has to learn to fit the mold. Because they are built on unconditional love, healthy rules contribute to everyone's self-esteem.

Healthy rules encourage change.

Healthy rules tend to be made for everyone's benefit. Everyone gets some protection from the rules. No one is left out or made to feel more at risk than any other person. In an unhealthy system, on the other hand, only the rule-maker benefits from the rules.

5. After rearranging the rules into the two lists and rewriting the ones which you want to change, make a separate list of all the healthy rules you have now compiled and by which you want to lead your life. These are your standards, precepts which for you are healthy and to which you knowingly subscribe. Display them in places about your home and workplace where you will be reminded of them often.

FOR REFLECTION AND DISCUSSION

1. What are some of the "shoulds" you experience in your family today?

2. Pick the two most important unhealthy rules in your lists and describe to someone else how these rules have brought unnecessary pain and confusion into your life.

3. Think about the problems giving up your unhealthy rules will create for you.

4. Who are the people you will disturb as you stop following the unhealthy rules? How will they try to encourage and/or coerce you back to your old patterns? What will you do to counter their negative influence?

5. How do you respond to George Crabbe's verse:
    Habit for him was all the test of truth;
    "It must be right:
       I've done it from my youth."

EXERCISE 17

SHOOTING YOURSELF IN THE FOOT: HOW YOU SABOTAGE YOUR OWN BEST INTERESTS

During our growing-up years, we developed negative ways of thinking and harmful patterns of behavior which helped us to survive the unhealthy atmosphere that surrounded our life. These strategies worked for us even though they were dysfunctional and self-destructive. They helped us to hide, to cover our fear or shame, and to cope with a world which threatened to overwhelm us. When we grew up and left our parents' home, we continued to practice these ways of thinking and feeling about ourselves and our environment. Because we do, we block ourselves from receiving the things we need for a wholesome and healthy life. We actually sabotage ourselves. Here are a few of the ways we shoot ourselves in the foot.

1) We ritualize frustrating patterns of relationships. (For example, we do the same "dance" every time we deal with a difficult person.)

2) We believe that others must agree and concede our point before it is safe for us to go on. (We cannot make a decision about our life unless our mate, child, or parent concurs.)

3) We jump to conclusions and make assumptions about what others are thinking and feeling. ("He doesn't like me." "She is mad at me.")

4) We make ourselves the center of the other person's world. (Whatever you do, you do because of me.")

5) We think that we owe every person an explanation for everything we do. (We must justify ourselves.)

6) We overgeneralize. ("This always happens to me." "Because this always happened in the past in this way, it will always happen this way in the future.")

7) We focus on the negative. ("My glass is always half empty." "I will lose, I know it." "They will like the other person better than me." "Someone else will get the job." "I'm not smart enough to go back to school.")

1) Select at least two of the previous seven negative tactics and in the space below write a brief example of how they apply to your life.

TACTIC #1

TACTIC #2

2) Think back during your years of growing up. Who modeled these behaviors for you? Did someone actually teach you to do these things to yourself? Who and how? Are you still practicing these destructive behaviors in order to get this person's love and approval? Write in your answers to these questions in the space below.

3) Rewrite each of the seven tactics so that it becomes a positive and healthy method of growth and self-development for you to use in your life.

FOR REFLECTION AND DISCUSSION

1. What were your feelings after you finished this
   exercise?

2. Think about how you are going to be different in the
   future because you understand how you complicate
   your own life and defeat yourself.

3. Ask a trusted friend to go over this list and tell you how
   they see you in relation to these self-destructive
   tendencies.

EXERCISE 18

THE MASKS WE HIDE BEHIND:
DEFENSE MECHANISMS
AND THE DIMINISHED PERSON

In order to alleviate the pain and anxiety of devaluation, diminished persons will frequently resort to irrational and self-destructive measures which have been called "ego defense mechanisms." These tactics are like masks which we use to hide reality from ourselves and from others. In the space provided below make a list of the masks which you wear. Next, compare your list with the following defense mechanisms and examples of how they work in the diminished person's life.

MECHANISM	EXAMPLE
DENIAL Screening out disagreeable realities.	Refusal to recognize the pain associated with continuing a relationship.
REPRESSION Preventing painful thoughts from entering consciousness. "Selective forgetting and remembering."	The consistent rage of the shamed person is denied access to awareness.
RATIONALIZATION Using contrived "explanations" to conceal unworthy motives for one's behavior.	The use of "I don't want to hurt ____" as justification for not telling the truth.
PROJECTION Attributing one's unacceptable motives to another.	An angry husband thinks that his wife is dissatisfied with him.
DISPLACEMENT Discharging hostile feelings on an object other than the one causing the feelings.	Shouting at the children when you are angry at your spouse.
EMOTIONAL INSULATION Reducing involvement by withdrawal and passivity.	Hiding feelings by refusing to acknowledge and feel feelings. Or, withdrawal.
UNDOING Attempting to atone for unacceptable desires and acts.	Feeling guilty about anger and trying to make up for it with sweetness and kindness.
OVERCOMPENSATION Covering up felt weakness by overemphasis on some desirable trait.	The insecure individual tries to appear super competent in every situation.

This exercise is designed to help you discover how you learned about defense mechanisms in your family and how you continue these practices today. Please answer the following questions:

1. The following are the defense mechanisms which my father seemed to use most frequently. (If you wish, you may think in terms of your father's present behavior rather than his behavior when you were a child.)

_____ An example:

_____ An example:

_____ An example:

2. The following are the defense mechanisms which my mother seemed to use most frequently. (As with your father, you may consider your mother's present behavior, if that is more useful for you.)

_____ An example:

_____ An example:

_____ An example:

3. The three defense mechanisms I use most are:

_____ An example:

_____ An example:

_____ An example:

REFLECTION AND DISCUSSION

1. How did you feel as you were thinking about and doing this exercise?

2. What are some more healthy ways for you to deal with your problems than hiding behind defense mechanisms?

3. One of the most dangerous defense mechanisms is denial, a tactic by which we refuse to see the reality of our situation. Have a trusted and safe person comment on your denial. Listen carefully and evaluate what this person says with an eye to how you may change. Talk with this person about how you may change and ways you can come out from your walls.

4. Consider the following cartoon. Does it say anything about your life?

CATHY
Copyright 1988 Universal Press Syndicate

EXERCISE 19

CREATIVE PLAYING:
HAVING FUN LIKE A KID AGAIN

When we are playing, and perhaps only when we are playing, we are free to be truly ourselves, unencumbered by the burdens of others' expectations and our own inhibitions and defenses. What is perhaps not so apparent is that a lot of what we call play is not really play. Organized sports for children and adults is called play. Most often it is not. Exercising and bodybuilding are sometimes referred to as playing. They can be, but most often they aren't. Partying, at which we practice some of the most painful aspects of our diminishment, is thought of as playing. It is not. Company socials and weekend relaxation are called play. Too often they are not. Watching television and other spectator games are sometimes thought of as play. Usually, they are not. Creative play, the play of the child, is something fundamentally different than these 20th century social habits.

Play is based on the willingness to let go. Letting go means that we are not measuring ourselves by the reactions of others. We are free of the obsessive need to win and competition, when present, is gentle and contributes to the quality of the game, not to any one person's ego. Creative play is not goal-directed in the sense that it has to have a worthy objective. It is its own reason for being. When we are really playing we are not taking ourselves too seriously like we do most of the time. Playing helps us to let go of that seriousness. Creative play, like all other worthy human pursuits is based on openness; openness to pleasure, to trust, to vulnerability, to lightness, and to growth and change. Creative play is based on our willingness to allow our inner child to come out and express herself or himself.

This exercise is designed to help you to let go, to let your child come out more, and to start really playing. Take a piece of paper and write three words on it:

Vocation
Relaxation
Relationships

Then write these words, "If I could do anything I wanted with my life, I would . . . ."

Next, close your eyes and imagine yourself stepping into an elevator. The doors close and you feel the elevator descend as you watch the numbers of each floor go by, beginning with ten and going to one. As each floor goes by, you feel yourself becoming more relaxed. When you reach the first floor, the doors open and you step out into the lobby of a beautiful hotel. Look at the fine furniture and the plush carpet, the beautiful art on the walls and the cut flowers that are placed about the room.

See yourself walking through the lobby and going out onto the street. There awaiting you is a limousine with driver. You get in and feel the automobile pull away from the curb. Let yourself feel the smoothness of the ride as you look out the window and see the sights as they go by.

Now the limousine stops and the driver announces that you are at your place of vocation. See yourself step out of the car and look about. You are at the place where you work, the place of satisfaction and fulfillment for you. This is your ideal job. You are happy here. Watch yourself walking about doing the job. See what you are doing. Feel the pleasure and be aware of what is making you feel so happy.

After a few minutes, it is time to go. You are once again in the limo. Let yourself feel the smooth ride and the power of the machine. Once more it stops and the driver announces that you are at your place of play. You step out and again you are supremely happy. You are relaxing and playing like a child. Watch yourself having fun and be aware of what you are doing. Know what is making you so happy.

Again, it is time to go. The car is moving and you are enjoying the ride. And again the driver stops the car and announces that you are at your place of relationships. You step out and are among your friends and those whom you love. You are very happy to be there and are enjoying the occasion very much. Be attentive to who is there and what you are doing with them. Why are you so happy?

Finally, it is time to go. You return to the car and arrive back at the hotel. See yourself walking through the lobby of the hotel. Look about again at the beautiful surroundings. Now you are on the elevator and going up. Watch the numbers as you ascend. You remain relaxed and comfortable. When you reach the tenth floor, the doors open and you step off. Take a couple of deep breaths and when you are ready, open your eyes.

After a few minutes for reflection, write down the important aspects of the experience you have just had. While you were doing this exercise, your unconscious mind was busy completing the sentence you started on the piece of paper. Without thinking about it and planning your answer, write out the completion of the sentence.

FOR REFLECTION AND DISCUSSION

1. What did the experience mean to you? What insights did you get about your work, your play, and your relationships?

2. Many people doing this exercise report that they were in the same place each time the limo stopped. In other words, they worked, played, and were with friends in the same place. Did you? What do you think this means about you?

3. Are there ways you can incorporate the kind of activities which you were doing in this imagery into your life? Write down some things you intend to do after gaining the insights of this exercise.

EXERCISE 20

WHAT ARE YOU TRYING TO GET?

All behavior is purposeful. Even the self-destructive behavior we engage in to avoid our pain has a purpose. Karen Horney, a famous therapist, was correct when she said that the result of a neurosis is its purpose. What that means is that we do all things for a reason. If we can stop and get a handle on what we are trying to accomplish in our "crazy" behavior, we can begin to get control of our lives and start changing the things we do that hurt us.

When we were children, we played one of a number of roles. Sharon Wegsheider-Cruse has identified four:

The Hero

Children (and adults) who play the hero child use perfection for self-protection. They are overachievers who have always been an adult. They are super-responsible. The family saddles them with taking care of the family honor. For healing, the hero (or the adult the hero grows into) needs self-acceptance. This child needs to feel, "It is okay for me to be me. I can be real and show the real me because I do not have to be perfect to be accepted by others."

The following are signs of the hero's recovery.
1. Asking for help instead of thinking we have to do it all.
2. Admitting a mistake to someone else and feeling comfortable.
3. Admitting negative feelings in ourselves or others.
4. Appreciating effort even if it fails.
5. Beginning to play, loosen up, not taking everything so seriously.

6. Turning down an honor that would overextend us. That is, being able to say, "No, thank you."

The Scapegoat

Children of this type act out negative behavior and hide themselves behind a wall of bravado. They are suspicious of everybody, even though no one may know it. The goal of their behavior is to protect themselves from other people, especially adults. For healing, a child of this type needs to learn to trust. She or he needs to learn to say, "I can be me because they are not going to hurt me. There is no need to protect myself from criticism and rejection by negative behavior." Scapegoat children and adults are getting better when:

1. We admit a mistake without blaming someone else.
2. We begin to accept the negative consequences of our behavior.
3. We start to develop a sense of humor about self.
4. We begin to perceive the difference between our wants and our needs.
5. If we have persisted in our acting-out behavior since childhood, we begin to give it up and to live in a more healthy way.

The Lost Child

Lost children use isolation as self-protection. They have real trouble knowing what they feel and let very little of their emotion show through. Because they have trouble even knowing what they feel, they imitate the feelings of others. They feel uninvolved, like they do not belong. For healing, this child must develop both trust and courage. She or he needs to be able to say, "I can come out of hiding and let people see me. I do not need to be afraid. I can let them see me."

When lost children start to recover, we:
1. Begin to identify our feelings.
2. Start talking and sharing our feelings.
3. Start showing feelings in the family, and with safe people outside the family.
4. Start beginning sentences with "I." This new way of speaking is the way to develop an identity and to build self-esteem.
5. Begin to ask that our needs be met. This new way of relating to ourselves and to others helps to give us a sense of control over ourselves and to have a better feeling about ourselves. Thus, it contributes to our growing self-esteem.

The Mascot

Mascot children are filled with anxiety and fear. They feel a lot of loneliness and try to placate others to cover over their pain. Children of this type are frequently hyperactive and often use humor, clowning, and being "cute" as ways of getting attention. They frequently grow up to be "pests," people who try to be funny but lack a sense of humor or who remain childish in their way of dress and speech patterns. They distract attention away from conflict and stress in the situation in order to keep the focus off what is really going on and what they are feeling. For healing this child needs a sense of self-control and responsibility. That is, he or she needs to say, "I can be real and I do not need to protect myself by keeping others happy, placated, and entertained. I can deal directly with what is going on and no longer must distract everybody by my endless activity."

Signs of recovery for the mascot include:
1. Developing a serious side that we allow to emerge in relationships.
2. Beginning to identify our own feelings and those of others correctly.
3. Talking about our feelings within close relationships.
4. Owning and taking responsibility for our feelings.
5. Having meaningful insights and sharing them.

1. After reading over the description of these various family roles, take some time to reflect on which one you played. You may find that you had a combination of two or more of the roles, that you played one role with some people and a different one with others, or that your role evolved from one to another through the years. Write out a brief description of you in the role(s) you played in your childhood family.

2. On a separate piece of paper, draw a *Family Role Map*. This map will not only show the roles each person played but will help you to symbolize the relationships within the family. Therefore, you will want to do two things: 1) Write in the names of each family member and significant person you want to include. Place the names on the page in such a way as to symbolize the relative distance between the various members and the way alliances between members existed. In other words, if father and sister were close, place their names close together. Be sure to include yourself. 2) After you have positioned all persons you intend to include in your family map, write out the role which each family member played beside their name. Then, beside your name draw a symbol of yourself and then draw a symbol of each other person.

3. Next, answer the following questions about your present role.

1. In what ways am I still playing today the role which I
   played in my childhood family?

2. How does this role hurt and limit me today and keep me from developing as a person?

3. What can I do that will help me to change this role? (Refer back to the signs of recovery discussed under each role.)

FOR REFLECTION AND DISCUSSION

1. What were your feelings as you did this exercise?

2. What insights did you gain about how you got to be the person you are today?

3. Many people feel very afraid when they think about giving up the major role they have played in significant groups. Do you have that feeling? What can you do about it?

4. As we recover from the dysfunctionalities of our childhood role, friends and relatives often pressure us to return to our old ways. Have you experienced that? What can you do about it?

5. Talk about the results of this exercise in your support group or share it with at least one safe person.

6. Consider and discuss in your group the following suggestions about the purposes of family roles:

1. They help us get *positive* attention. What we feel is, "I'm only important when I'm getting positive attention." The problem is that if we are not okay until we get the positive attention, the role can be overwhelming. How about an attitude which says, "I'll be okay even if you do not like me."

2. Or, they help us get *negative* attention. We say, "Since I can't get positive attention, I'll be important by getting negative attention." Children blocked in some way from getting positive attention will often resort to

this tactic of attention-getting. Second children will frequently become the scapegoat when the first child is a hero. In any case, when our family is sick, we resort to sick ways of getting attention. Sometimes people will switch back and forth between negative and positive attention-getters.

3. Roles are always related to *power* in the family. "I only feel important when I am in control of others or at least when I can keep them from controlling me." This is the purpose of little children when they refuse to talk. Adults do it when they have to have their way. Some families have ongoing power struggles that are never resolved. The whole family revolves around the battle. If you are in a power struggle that you do not want, withdraw. Control yourself, not the other person, by abandoning the fight.

4. Roles sometimes are about *revenge*. What we are saying in effect is, "I've been hurt so much, I can only be important by hurting others and getting even." This is a kind of vampire logic which is designed to hurt before being hurt.

5. Other times roles help us get *compensation* for our pain. We compensate ourselves by taking care of others. We seem to say, "I've been hurt so much, I'm only important when I keep other people from hurting when I hurt." We make a martyr of ourselves.

6. Finally, some roles are designed to *display inadequacy*. What we portray in our actions is, "There is no way I can ever be important, so I give up. Leave me alone." We isolate and our "lostness" both conceals and dramatizes our pain and fear.

EXERCISE 21

ENCOUNTER:
HOW TO BE INTIMATE
WITHOUT LOSING YOURSELF

Diminished people have trouble with intimacy. We want love and seek it sometimes to the point of an addiction. Yet when the opportunity for genuine intimacy appears, we get afraid and run away. Thus, we want it and yet are afraid of it. We also lack what may be called "intimacy skills." We do not really know how to establish and maintain intimate relationships either with members of the opposite sex or with our own. Further, we are not intimate with ourselves. That is, we lack the basic ingredient of intimacy, a developed self-identity that we *like*.

This exercise is designed to help us begin the process of looking at how our diminishment robs us of what may be the most satisfying of all human experiences, genuine intimacy with other human beings.

1. Let's begin with a brief personal reflection. First, spend some time with a few words of the vocabulary of intimacy. As you reflect on the following words, look for memories, flashes of insight, and images. Allow yourself to respond to these words and allow them to become real to you.

Friendship
Commitment
Teamwork
Openness
Love
Isolation
Sexuality

Loneliness
Competition
Loss
Rejection and Abandonment

2. Return now to one of the words, one that was especially meaningful to you because it produced a wide range of memories and feelings for you. Write the word in this blank. _____ If more than one word leaped out at you, write in the other words also.

3. Write briefly what the word means to you and the memories and feelings that are associated with it for you.

4. What does this experience say about your strengths and skills in intimacy?

5. How do your memories and feelings in this exercise help you recognize what limits you in intimate relationships?

6. What are the specific areas in which you need to change to *be* with others?

FOR REFLECTION AND DISCUSSION

1. How did you feel as you did this exercise?

2. Discuss what this exercise means to you in your support group or with at least one safe person.

3. Do you feel that you are being intimate as you share your memories and feelings that this exercise brought up?

Part Four

GROWING UP TO BE YOU IN THE DAYS AHEAD

The following exercises are designed to help us think about where we want to go with our lives in the days ahead. We have spent a lot of time in the previous pages with both our past and our present. Now we turn our eyes to the future and the rest of our life. We are not, of course, finished with the past nor are we now unconcerned with the present issues. We will return to them both many times as we continue our journey in the days ahead. But in the earlier exercises, we have made a start in dealing with these matters and have laid a good foundation upon which we can begin to plan where we want to go from here.

These exercises are intended to help us organize our life in such a way as to know what we want. Being aware of what we want is a big step in the process of accomplishing what we want. You may do as much with each suggested exercise as you wish. That is, you may do each of them as a brief exercise that only takes a few minutes. Or, you may spend several hours working on each step of the process. How extensive you go into each topic is a matter of personal decision.

Please do not skip any of the exercises and do them in sequence. Remember also, nothing is written in concrete. Despite what you write on these pages, you will surely change your mind as you proceed through the years ahead.

EXERCISE 22

THE PAST LINE AND
THE WIWTDWTROML LINE:
YOUR LIFE FROM START TO FINISH

1. In the middle of the space below, write the year of your birth at the left margin of the page. Write today's date opposite it at the right hand side of the page. Next, draw a line from one date to the other. This line represents your life from the time of your birth to the present. You may call it your PAST LINE.

Next, divide the line between these two dates into five-year intervals that represent the half-decades of your life. Now, think about the important events that happened to you in each of these five-year periods. Write them into the appropriate space. Write the positive ones above the line and the negative ones below the line. How far you place them from the line can symbolize the degree to which they are positive or negative for you. Try to be as complete as possible. If you need more space than is allowed, feel free to use another piece of paper.

2. You are ready now to do a WIWTDWTROML LINE. That is, you may now do a "What I want to do with the rest of my life" line. To do this, take another piece of paper and at the bottom of the page at the left margin, write today's date. Then at the top of the page at the right margin write "The Finish Line." Draw a line between these two. Your line should run diagonally across the page from the bottom to the top. This is your WIWTDWTROML LINE.

Next, write in along this line the things you really *want* to do with your life. Do not let yourself be inhibited by others' expectations, by your own pessimism, or the feeling of limitations. There should, of course, be an effort to stay with reality. But within that boundary, let your imagination go. What are the things you would really do with yourself if you were *completely* free to do whatever you wanted? Again, be as complete and as detailed as possible. You may wish to arrange the entries chronologically up the line. Or, if you prefer, you may write down on another sheet of paper what comes to your mind in the order that they come to you and then transpose them to the WIWTDWTROML LINE in your preferred chronological sequence.

3. Now you are ready to deal with your GOALS. On the basis of the things you have written on these pages answer the following questions.

1) What are five strengths I have?

2) What are five weaknesses I have?

3) What are three things I fear happening to me?

4) Overall, what is the one thing I want my life to accomplish?

5) Overall, what are my goals?

FOR REFLECTION AND DISCUSSION

1. How did you feel as you were doing this exercise?

2. Consider your PAST LINE. What do you see there? Are there any surprises for you? Do you see any patterns? What important things come to you as you look at these materials? On a separate piece of paper, write out at least five things that you observe about the person this life line describes.

3. Now turn your attention to the WIWTDWTROML LINE. Are there any surprises for you on this page? What kind of person does this page reveal you to be? What would you say your basic values are as revealed by this page? Will you be satisfied with your life if you accomplish at least some of these things? Which ones? What is there about those things which make them so important?

4. As you think about the results of this exercise and as you contemplate Exercise 23, consider Margaret Lee Runbeck's comment, "Happiness is not a state to arrive at, but a manner of traveling."

EXERCISE 23

PLANNED HAPPINESS INVENTORY

PART I

List five things you *really* wish to do with your life before you die. These are things which are deep but real desires. Do not be limited by what you think others expect of you or even by what you think is "reasonable." These may be little things (I want to camp out in the Canadian Rockies) or big things (I want to own my own camping store). Do not limit yourself by the statement, "I shouldn't put that down because I could never do it." The only rule here is that it be something you want for yourself.

1.

2.

3.

4.

5.

PLANNED HAPPINESS INVENTORY

PART II

List at least two strengths which you have that will help you to accomplish each of the items you have written above.

Item 1

  1. _____

  2. _____

Item 2

  1. _____

  2. _____

Item 3

  1. _____

  2. _____

Item 4

  1. _____

  2. _____

Item 5

  1. _____

  2. _____

Describe the specific reward, joy, or sense of fulfillment you think you will receive as you accomplish each of these things you wish for your life.

Item 1

Item 2

Item 3

Item 4

Item 5

PLANNED HAPPINESS INVENTORY

PART III

List the factors which keep you from achieving or at least attempting each of the items listed above.

Item 1

Item 2

Item 3

Item 4

Item 5

FOR REFLECTION AND DISCUSSION

1. Go back and compare what you have written in this exercise with what you wrote in the previous one. How are they different? In what ways are they similar.

2. What will you do differently in your life to accomplish these goals?

3. Were you surprised with any of the strengths or weaknesses which you wrote about?

4. How do you plan to emphasize your strengths and to improve on your weaknesses?

5. Share in your group or with one safe person what this exercise meant to you.

EXERCISE 24

THE CONCLUSION

The following exercise is an adaptation of some suggestions from Anthony deMello's book *Wellsprings*.
deMello begins his book with "The Conclusion," a reflection in which the reader is invited to consider at the start
where he or she wants to come out in the end. Make yourself comfortable and get in a relaxed state. You may wish
to turn the lights down and put on some soft instrumental
music. Unplug the phone and make sure that no one will
disturb you. When you are ready, let your mind roam
across the following statements. Reflect quietly and deeply on them, letting your mind go back and forth across
them until you are satisfied that you have thought them
through.

I imagine that today I am to die.

I ask for time to be alone in order to write down for my
friends a sort of testament for which the points that follow
would serve as chapter titles.

1) These are the things I have loved in life:
   Sights
   Sounds
   Smells
   Tastes
   Touches

2) These are the ideas that have liberated me.

3) These are the convictions by which I have lived.

4) These are the risks I took, the dangers I courted.

5) These are the things I have suffered.

6) These are the things I regret about my life.

7) These are my achievements.

8) These are my unfulfilled dreams.

FOR REFLECTION AND DISCUSSION

1. How did it feel to contemplate your own death?

2. Which of the "chapters" was most evocative for you? Why do you think this aspect of your life was so interesting to you at this point?

3. Were there any surprises for you? Did you learn anything about yourself?

4. What do you plan to do differently in your life as a result of this exercise?

EXERCISE 25

POLICIES AND PROCEDURES FOR ME

Everyone needs a rule of life which can serve as his or her own personal policy statement. Businesses have policies and procedures and these written documents help in the decision-making process. The following are a suggested list of precepts which may be useful to help you write out your own set of policies for guiding your life. Consider them and then amend them in any way which makes sense to you.

I. I will not fret. Fretting is an extreme form of worry and worry is the most unproductive of all human activities.

II. I will not be ruled by fear. Most of the things we fear never come to pass.

III. I will count my blessings, never overlooking the small ones. A lot of small blessings add up to a big one and sometimes the small ones are best of all.

IV. I will not expect to live free of problems. No worthy life is ever problem-free. I will handle each as it comes and no more than one at a time.

V. When I am tied up in a knot, exhausted, irritable or out of sorts, I will rest.

VI. I will not lie or cover up the truth.

VII. I will not rescue or fix other human beings or save them from the negative consequences of their actions.

VIII. I will not cross bridges before I get to them. No one yet has succeeded in accomplishing this feat.

IX. I will try to be a good listener. Only when I listen do I hear ideas other than my own. It is very hard to learn something new when I am the one doing all the talking.

X. I will not become bogged down with bitterness. When I express my anger in words, it evaporates, like steam from a kettle. When I hold it in, it finally explodes. I will not let frustrations build up and interfere with positive action.

FOR REFLECTION AND DISCUSSION

1. How do you feel as you read over these "rules"?

2. Does any one of them stand out for you?

3. Do you wish to revise them in any way?

4. Are there any important topics for you that were left out of the list?

EPILOGUE

When we follow the pathways of recovery, we grow into normal, healthy adults who are able to know our feelings and to express them directly to appropriate persons. We learn how to admit our problems to ourselves and talk about them with others. We have a sense of competence and experience ourselves as in control of our lives and adequate in dealing with our immediate world. We grow out of the dependency and limitations of the diminished child.

We put the past in its proper place. In our emotional, cognitive, and behavioral worlds, we have lived in the past at the mercy of other people. Most of the time, we felt like a child in our relationships with others, especially in our close and more intimate relationships. That is, we saw ourselves as weak and dependent, needy and unable to express ourselves freely or fully. We give up these feelings as we travel toward wholeness. We are free to be aware of our feelings and to express them in words, behavior, and other ways. What's more, we are beginning to expect others to do the same.

Before we started this journey, we often felt like strangers in our own home and were so fearful that we had trouble making conversation. We had difficulty knowing what we needed and were dependent on the signals of others to perceive what was expected of us. When we were with other people, we often felt that we were being deprived of something and that something was missing. Sexual relations were like a performance for us and more times than not we felt more like an outsider observing our performance than an actual participant.

We had a great need for approval which we construed as tenderness and gentleness. We needed others to be considerate of us and could not stand even the hint of conflict. Because we were so afraid of rejection, we became masters at manipulation, passive aggression, and deception to get what we wanted without directly asking for it.

Our lack of personal value, along with our inordinate fear of rejection, caused us to develop a service-oriented mentality. We became expert in taking care of others. But our ministrations were not really predicated on our sincere and genuine interest in them. Rather, they were based on the vain hope that if we were "nice" to others, they would give us approval in return. Our tragedy was that we truly felt that if we were ourselves, and only ourselves without some "extra" performance or quality, those people from whom we needed love would have nothing to do with us.

But now we are on a different track. This book has taken us through a number of exercises which have helped us understand how we were diminished and what to do about it. We are moving away from the dependency and awkwardness of the wounded child in us and toward the competent, sensitive, loving, and responsible adult that child was originally designed to be.

The question now is, "Where do we go from here and how do we keep on track?" That is the question of our last exercise.

EXERCISE 26

WHERE DO WE GO FROM HERE
or
HOW TO WIN OUT OVER DIMINISHMENT

Our goal in all these exercises has been to construct a foundation upon which we may continue to build. The following are concrete things we can do in our life, starting today, which will help us to continue to overcome the shame, fear, and doubt that we allowed to rule us since childhood.

1. Continue to seek understanding. We must use the principles we have learned here to continue to look into our life to find how and in what ways we have been diminished. We can read, talk to others, join a group in our unrelenting insistence on personal growth.

2. Do the grief work that is necessary. Grief is necessary to growth. We lost our childhood and we lost many aspects of a happy adulthood. These are gone forever and grieving them is necessary. We can also remember that one very important part of grief is anger. Some anger is necessary as we grieve the losses which our diminishment has forced upon us.

3. We can become more willing to make changes.

We can change our self-talk, the inner conversation that we have with ourselves.

We can learn more rational responses to stressful situations.

We can begin to restructure all our relationships in more healthy ways.

We can learn to give up deception and become more honest first with ourselves and then with others.

We can learn better communication habits.

4. Detachment with love will be necessary. It will be difficult but we can start to give up control of the other people in our life.

5. We must not overlook our spiritual growth. In fact, all of recovery is in reality no more than the process of spiritual growth.

6. We can keep on practicing. Life is a journey and it is made one step at a time. We can stop our discouragement with "slow progress" or lack of perfection. Let's keep our destination in mind and move toward it one day at a time.

FOR REFLECTION AND DISCUSSION

As you complete this last exercise and take leave of this book, consider the following affirmations. You may wish to pick one a day and make it your guiding principle for that day. Write your name in the blank and go about your daily activities repeating the statement to yourself.

LOVING ME/BEING ME

1. I, _____, am a complete person, capable of loving and open relationships.

2. I, _____, have all the things I need to make me a happy, growing person.

3. I, _____, am attracting people into my life who are loving and healthy.

4. I, _____, have a lot of love inside me that I can give easily and thus makes me able to love both myself and others.

5. I, _____, think highly of myself and therefore it is easy for me to accept others thinking highly of me.

6. I, _____, am learning to state my feelings rather than judge my friends and their feelings.

7. I, _____, am beginning to feel that I deserve being loved.

8. I, _____, am completely in charge of my feelings, thoughts, and action.

9. I, _____, am beginning to think and talk positively and I am attracting into my life people who think and talk positively.

10. I, _____, am learning that it is what I do with *today* that counts.

11. As I, _____, learn to take responsibility for myself, I have more mutual and honest relationships.

12. I, _____, am not destroyed when other people do not understand or accept my behavior.

13. I, _____, am a responsible person who is happy and free and worthy of all the good things life has to offer.